ARGUING WITH FRIENDS

Keeping your friends and your convictions

Paul Buller

August 2012

ISBN: 1478395028
ISBN-13: 978-1478395027

DEDICATION

This book is dedicated to the guys in my philosophy group with whom I have made many of the mistakes I describe. Thank you for your ceaseless grace in light of my obvious, and sometimes frequent, shortcomings.

This book is also dedicated to armchair scholars everywhere who discuss more important subjects than traffic, weather and sports. Keep the conversation alive!

After I ventured my opinion we got in to a long argument and became firm friends.
Irving Hexham (personal blog)

TABLE OF CONTENTS

An overview of the training program

It has been said,

"If I profess, with the loudest voice and the clearest exposition, every portion of the truth of God except precisely that little point which the world and the devil are at that moment attacking, I am not confessing Christ, however boldly I may be professing Christianity. Where the battle rages the loyalty of the soldier is proved; and to be steady on all the battle-field besides is mere flight and disgrace to him if he flinches at that one point." [1]

Strong words. In essence, to truly spread the message of Christ in our world, our culture, our time, there is an element of battle. We may not like that idea, but the Bible even describes it in such militant terms.[2] In fact, not only is spiritual battle something to be endured - when it happens upon us, quite accidentally - we ought to seek it out! How many of us get excited at the prospect of sharing our deepest convictions if we know, full well, that sharing them with others will plant us firmly at the front lines of spiritual warfare?

---

[1] This quote has been attributed to Martin Luther, though a brief internet search suggests this may be a false attribution - **http://creation.com/battle-quote-not-luther**. Although Martin Luther may not have said this, he almost certainly would have endorsed it.

[2] This is a major theme of Ephesians 6:10-20, for instance.

Honestly, it's not my first choice. The preference of many is toward tolerance and bridge-building, not divisions and battle lines. Is there truly a role for spiritual "warfare?" Can it be done... shall we say... peaceably?

We have all seen conversations like these go very badly and many of us assume such outcomes are inevitable. Some people charge into the discussion with all the grace of a bull in a China shop. Others clam up and change the subject as tactfully as possible. Many will speak in vague generalities that could never possibly offend anybody. But if we do allow ourselves to be "pinned down" on this issue or that, the battle begins.

Often times these conversations end with misunderstandings, raised voices and tears. Family gatherings just aren't the same again, are they? Church meetings end in brokenness and disillusionment. Even if we want to discuss the issues, many of us fear losing friends just by bringing up the subject or sharing our views when somebody else brings up the subject. When discussing these matters with others it seems we are faced with a choice; either we keep our friends (by hiding our convictions), or we share and defend our views (and lose our friends). Many people think it is impossible to stand your ground and keep your friends. How did we get into this mess?

The purpose of this book is to give you an overview of how to navigate difficult subjects - especially standing up for your Christian faith - with greater success. Even though this book is written from a Christian perspective, with an eye on sharing your faith with others, the principles apply equally well to just about any difficult conversation you might have on any subject.

I used to think that the biggest problem with the world today was that not enough people knew the Truth. I now believe the problem runs deeper than that; most people have trouble identifying Truth in the first place, and more specifically, testing for error. We may think a lot, but we have not learned how to think well. This is part of the reason why we keep getting scam emails; there are enough people out there who will fall for the scams to motivate the scammers to keep trying. In fact, scamming remains such a successful industry that I have started getting snail-mail scam letters and even phone scammers! Too many people have lost the skill of properly analyzing claims as I will describe in greater depth later.

It gets worse. Many people have also lost the fine art of communication. Even if somebody has a handle on the Truth, they would have a hard time passing that on to others with clarity. What a double-whammy against society as a whole; we are ill-equipped to find Truth in the first place, and if we happen to stumble upon it we haven't developed the skills to point others in the right direction. How can we ever hope to spread the Truth with these two strikes against us? You can use some of the strategies outlined in this book to help those who have trouble differentiating truth from error to see things more clearly. Furthermore, with some practice you will learn to better articulate yourself by ensuring your thoughts are clear and reasonable. You will be better equipped to navigate the sea of options, find Truth and share that with others more effectively.

Given what I consider to be the more fundamental problem with society, this book will not stock you up with a bunch of "right answers." Phase 5 will show you where to look for information on various subjects; that's your homework for when you are done reading this book. Also, this book is not a detailed step-by-step manual for navigating these kinds of discussions. Every conversation is different, so it is rather presumptuous to think that I can tell you exactly what to do in any given situation. This book will help you understand, at a high level, what separates a successful conversation from an unsuccessful one, and give you some general strategies for these kinds of dialogues to increase your odds of success. Most importantly, though, this book will guide you through the extensive training it takes to develop these skills; training that should take years.

Why do I call it "Arguing" with friends? Shouldn't I have found a less confrontational word? We need to better understand the real meaning of the word "Argument," instead of the quarreling, antagonistic misunderstanding.[3] Any time we explain and defend our views we are "arguing" for our viewpoint, much like a lawyer argues in defense of his/her client. In this

[3] Monty Python illustrates this beautifully - **http://youtu.be/hnTmBjk-M0c**

sense, an "argument" is nothing more than explaining our beliefs and the reasons behind them. There's nothing offensive or quarrelsome about that, is there? Learning how to argue well will help us keep our friends, and will also help us learn to discern whether other people are sharing the Truth, or trying to pull a fast one on you.

The most important question of this book is this: what does success look like? That may seem obvious; I succeed if I change the other person's mind.

Wrong answer! Consider this; what if the other person is right and you are wrong? In that case you have just led somebody astray when you should have followed their direction. Furthermore, when people are focused on changing somebody else's mind they often become very heavy-handed in the process, or sometimes they start "cutting corners," even ethical corners, to accomplish their goal. Strange as it may seem, changing the other person's mind should never be your ultimate goal.

Ok, so the more general goal would seem to be truth itself, right? A successful conversation of significance is when both people move closer to truth.

Most of the time these conversations end without anybody changing their mind, which means (by that definition) we fail about 99% of the time. When a person comes to Jesus that usually takes a very long time and a lot of conversations. Success for us has nothing to do with conversion. At first that might sound blasphemous, but it is actually Biblical.[4] Too often we take the weight of God's job and put it on our shoulders which is why so many people are downright frightened by the very idea of Evangelism. We need to do our job and God will do his. Success does not depend on anybody changing their mind in any particular conversation.

---

[4] John 6:44 gives a clear picture of God's active role in Salvation. Also, reference the book of Acts where it claims that "the Lord added to their number..." (i.e. Acts 2:47, 11:21) Consider that it highlights "the Lord" as the cause of their increase, as opposed to "they added to their own number..."

Here's what I believe is the definition of a successful conversation: when both people have clearly articulated and defended their beliefs with mutually respectful dialogue. The focus of success is not the result of the conversation, but the conversation itself. If they understood each other, that is success! If they are eager to start the conversation again, feeling as though they have deepened their friendship with the other person, that is success! If anybody changes their mind, that should be a side-effect of success, not the goal.

> *Success in witnessing is communicating Christ in the power of the Holy Spirit and leaving the results to God. Similarly, effectiveness in apologetics is presenting cogent and persuasive arguments for the Gospel in the power of the Holy Spirit, and leaving the results to God*
>
> ***William Lane Craig***

This book uses the metaphor of athletic training. Think of this as a multi-phase training regime, and the stations are individual workouts. Some of the training is "on the job" and some of it needs to be done ahead of time.

Why do I use the exercise metaphor? As I mentioned, most people (at least in Canada where I live) are completely out of shape when it comes to discerning and sharing Truth through civil discourse. Many people are completely unable to explain their perspective in a coherent manner.[5] Some avoid talking about these things at all. Many people think that "success" is measured by the strength of your bullying technique. A lot of these problems stem from the fact that many people are intellectually out of shape; we need to understand what the word "argument" really means and how to effectively utilize Reason to discern and describe Truth. We need to work off the fat of lazy thinking and increase our mental agility and preparedness.

To get you on the path toward better conversational fitness, here is a breakdown of the training program.

Phase 1 - Pre-season training. This is stuff that you should work through before you get into too many conversations.

---

[5] This young lady provides a particularly vivid example of the difficulty some people have of presenting their ideas in a coherent manner.
http://youtu.be/U5oVzbwYWpg

Phase 2 - Strategies for success. We can never guarantee success, but we can increase the odds through effective strategies.

Phase 3 - Learn from the mistakes of others. Mistakes happen; try to avoid them by understanding them first.

Phase 4 - Successful failures. Conversations do not always go well; here are some ways to deal with the good, bad and ugly.

Phase 5 - Specific subjects to study. If knowledge is power, then here are some areas to study to increase your power. By this stage you should have a better idea of how to handle your "power" with gentleness and respect.

Please, for the love of your friendships, do not skip ahead to Phase 5 without going through the first four. The temptation may be strong to dive into the "Christian answers" to all those tough questions but that proves far more damaging than helpful without having first learned how to deliver the facts.

Lastly I want to point out that this book is merely intended to open the door to success, not chauffeur you all the way there. You will notice this book is rather light-weight; it was intended to be so. This book will merely open the door and briefly survey the landscape for the reader who may never have previously thought about these matters. It would be well worth the effort for you to read the other books in the Bibliography to continue you along your journey because I certainly do not cover everything relevant to this subject (though I believe I hit most of the key points). And, of course, practical experience is imperative. You can read all the theory you like, but until you step out into the real world and have real conversations like these, you will not actually know how to implement these skills. Go for it, try what you learn here, fail, get up, apologize if you need to and try again.

Phase 1 – Pre-season training

When I first got interested in Christian Apologetics I was, frankly, an embarrassment because I did not have any good examples to follow and nobody taught me how to do it correctly.[6] I lost a few friends in the early years, and I imagine a few other people may have been delayed on their journey to Truth because of my behavior. Many of the lessons of this book are rooted in mistakes I made that I had to learn my own way out of because I had nobody to mentor me and I was unaware of books like this one. I am still far from perfect, but I know I have made many significant gains. Of course, it wasn't easy. The hard work that I lay out in this book is just a starting point for you to chisel away some of your own "fat" and start developing skills in dialogue and Reason in preparation for having good, healthy, discussions with people.

Are you ready for the pre-season training? Let's go!

Station 1 - What's the point of talking?

Before you get into the conversation, consider your motives carefully. And I don't mean the motives you tell somebody if they ask, but the motives you

[6] Some examples of mistkaes are listed here - **http://www.apologetics315.com/2012/01/10-pitfalls-of-foolish-apologist.html**

carry deep in your heart. I never used to admit it, but I really wanted people to be impressed with my stunning intellect. For me, it was about showing my mastery of Reason, Philosophy and rhetorical skills; I wanted to impress them with my stunning intellect. Even today such delusions of grandeur still hover in my soul, but I have successfully "pushed past" it so that it does not (usually!) impact the conversation.

You need to do similar reflection. Consider carefully why you are getting into these conversations. The biggest mistake that people make is to personalize the conversation. I want to look smart. I want to be right. I want to win. Me, me, me. The real purpose needs to be truth, and that has little to do with you. You need to get used to the taste of humble pie.

In an ideal conversation your job is to share the Truth in such a way that the focus of the conversation is Truth and not you, or your friend. In one sense you need to dialogue in such a way as to take yourself out of the equation. Consider carefully the difference between these two attitudes:

- My **BELIEFS** are true

- **MY** beliefs are true

Both say the same thing, but the first attitude focuses on the Truth, and the second focuses on you as the holder of Truth. Never forget the point of conversation: **it's about Truth, and not about you**. Get over yourself.[7]

Station 2 - Know your strengths and weaknesses

Did you ever notice how long-distance runners and sprinters have very different physical builds? Those who run for a long time at a medium speed have far less muscle mass than do those who sprint at top speed for a short distance. Could a sprinter do well in a 1K event? Probably not. How would

[7] In the lecture series Apologetics Survey, Dr. Groothuis quotes Socrates (Lecture 7, 24:30; see Bibliography) "The point of an argument is not for one person to win or the other person to win; it is for truth to win through rationality."

an endurance runner do if competing against Usain Bolt in a 100m dash? Very poorly, obviously.

Just as athletes have different physical builds, so God has created us all differently. This is why a one-size-fits-all book on the nuts and bolts of these kinds of conversations probably isn't best. I cannot tell you exactly how to tackle these subject, that's for you and God to figure out based on whoever you are talking to. Here are three broad questions to consider.

- What are my strengths?

- What are my weaknesses?

- Which of my weaknesses need to be corrected?

Imagine you are training for an endurance event. You assess that your strength area is that you can keep on going and going like the energizer bunny. However, you do not have a lot of muscle mass. Well, that weakness, combined with that strength, is just about perfect for an endurance event. It would be unwise to "correct" for the weakness of not having a lot of muscle mass. Personally, I feel fairly comfortable discussing subjects such as theology, philosophy and general science. I'm not so good with history and I find the details about some aspects of science - like Quantum Physics - rather difficult to grasp. Based on this, I am able to easily carry on certain conversations, and God has used that in a number of situations.

But not all weaknesses are "just who I am." Suppose one of your weaknesses is that you are profoundly lazy. Well, that's going to make it difficult to compete in either the endurance running or sprinting competitions. That's a weakness that needs to be corrected, not worked around. From my own background, I had a problem with raising the volume (and the blood pressure) on conversations when somebody didn't see things my way. That was also a weakness but that one definitely needed correcting.

So some weaknesses are an indication of which skills God wants to hone in your life, and other weaknesses are simply spiritual problems that need correcting. Here are some questions to ask yourself; these reflect certain common shortcomings of people when they engage in the conversation.

- How easy are you to talk to when you are hungry / tired / stressed, etc?

- Do you get easily angered? Do you shy away from controversy? What is your personality type?

- Which subjects are you most comfortable with? Which subjects are beyond your ability to understand?

- Can you feel your heart pounding as soon as a disagreement surfaces? Do you take "confrontation" personally? Does it excite you?

Take some time to do an honest self-assessment and make the changes (with God's guidance and assistance) where they need to be made. On some issues - perhaps you are difficult to talk to when you are hungry - that may not need changing, but you should time your conversations accordingly. Just remember, there is no such thing as a one-size-fits-all Christian; **don't change what does not need changing!** This will help you ensure that you do the best job possible in these conversations, while avoiding the common pitfalls that ruin friendships in the process.

Station 3 - Critical Thinking

Logic. How profoundly boring! What a ridiculous waste of time, right? Wouldn't you rather watch paint dry? Hear me on this one: I don't think it is any exaggeration to say that one of the biggest reasons why so many people don't know how to effectively communicate without losing their friends is because they don't know the basics of logic (I will discuss this much more in Phase 4). That's right, this ridiculously boring subject may just help people learn to talk with each other without the gloves coming off.

Logic is one of the primary tools we use to figure out if something is even possibly true or not. Even if you don't realize it, you use logic all the time! The challenge is to learn to use it well, like a sprinter needs to learn to run well, even if most people are capable of running. If you use Logic poorly then you risk holding firmly to false beliefs because they seem true.

Consider this example. We all know that dogs have four legs. Your friend bought a dog and you want to get them a Christmas present for their dog. You decide to get them those cute little animal slippers. How many to buy? Well, obviously four, right? You know the answer even if you've never met their new pet and counted the legs.

Without realizing it, you just used logic. It went like this:[8]

P1 - Dogs have four legs
P2 - My friend bought a dog, therefore
C1 - My friend's dog has four legs

["P" means "Premise" and "C" means "Conclusion"]

Well, that's pretty obvious, really. Yes it is; Logic takes common sense from everyday life and helps you understand why it makes sense. It can also help you understand why some ways of thinking are wrong. Suppose instead that you met your friend in the mall and they had just bought those cute little slippers for their pet. Now you didn't know they bought a pet and they didn't mention what kind of animal it was. You see the four slippers and you congratulate them on buying a dog. They look at you kind of funny and explain that they bought a cat.

Oops; what went wrong? Well, you made an error in logic that went like this.

P1 - Dogs have four legs
P2 - My friend's pet has four legs, therefore

---

[8] For the really astute reader, even this formulation is not quite logically perfect. I'm trying to strike a balance between accuracy and readability. Please forgive me.

C1 - My friend's pet is a dog

Nope, that doesn't work. This error is called, "Affirming the Consequent." There are four possible pieces of information you can have in this little example, but only two of them can be used to deduce another, related, fact.

1) It is a dog --> We can conclude it has four legs
2) It is not a dog --> We cannot draw any conclusions about how many legs it has (it could be a gorilla or a centipede).
3) It has four legs --> We cannot draw any conclusions about whether it is a dog or not. If we did, that would be the logical error of "Affirming the Consequent," as mentioned previously.
4) It does not have four legs --> We can conclude it is not a dog.

Notice how (1) and (4) are logically valid and (2) and (3) are not. You don't need to memorize this particular set of examples, but hopefully this helps you see how taking the time to understand some of these rules, and making the right kinds of connections between concepts, will help you avoid making these mistakes. Perhaps equally importantly, knowing some of these rules will help you avoid being misled by other people. For instance, I tell you that if God does not exist then a lightening bolt will not come down from the sky and strike me dead if I insult him. Hey, look, no lightening bolt came down from the sky to strike me dead when I insulted him so, obviously, God does not exist. Well, let's look at that.

P1 - If God does not exist then I will not be struck with lightning when I insult him.

P2 - I did not get struck with lightning when I insulted him, therefore

C1 - God does not exist.

Compare this one to the previous example of Affirming the Consequent and you should be able to see that the same formulation of the error exists in both. Knowing how to reformulate these kinds of discussions into logical form, and knowing how to spot what is called a logical fallacy can help you make sure your own ideas are logical, and avoid being misled by somebody else who makes logical mistakes. For further reading on this subject, I highly recommend the book, "A Rulebook for Arguments" (see the Bibliography for details).

Laws of Thought

Mistakes that people make in logic will be discussed in more detail later. For now I want to highlight some "laws of thought" that are foundational to successful reasoning and dialogue. These Laws were discovered centuries ago and have stood the test of time. These form the basis of all use of Reason, including the examples I just went through.

Law of Identity - This law is somewhat abstract in its pure form, but I think a version of it is very useful for any conversation. It is essentially this; make sure you are using terms consistently, clearly and correctly. When you talk about "Church," for instance, you may need to clarify if you are referring to the global Body of Christ - as in "all believers everywhere" - or if you mean that specific group of people that you worship with on Sunday mornings. A great many communication failures can be traced to lack of clarity in the use of words, or equivocating on their definitions. Always take time to clarify with people, "what do you mean when you say..." and make sure you are clear on what you mean as well.

And, of course, make sure that your understanding is correct. In summary, get your facts straight and describe them with clarity!

Law of Non-Contradiction - I think this is a very intuitive law. If I make some claim about reality, then I am also claiming (even if I don't explicitly say so) that the opposite is false. For instance, if I tell you that "I am older than 30" and then I tell the person beside you that "I am NOT older than 30" you would immediately recognize that something is wrong. If I claim that the Japanese attack on Pearl Harbor occurred on December 17, 1941, and a history-buff friend of mine says that it did NOT occur on December 17, 1941 then it is impossible for us to both be right. Two contradictory claims cannot both be correct; in this case my friend would be right.

Law of Excluded Middle - In my mind this is closely related to the Law of Non-Contradiction and simply says that either some claim is true, or its opposite is true. Either I have, with me, enough spare change to pay for bus fare, or I do not. There is no third option. How the Law of Excluded Middle applies in everyday life can get confusing. For instance, when deciding where to go for dinner, there are usually many more than just two options. In the cases where many options exist, the Law of Excluded Middle does not directly apply. However, even in that case, if I have my heart set on Chinese food and my wife does not (as is typically the case) then we are either going to go to a restaurant that serves Chinese food, or we are not, there is no third option. If we end up going to a restaurant that does not serve Chinese food (as is also typically the case) then a world of other choices opens up; pasta, burgers, East Indian, etc. The Law of Excluded Middle only applies when you are dealing with "A, or not A" types of situations. Those situations emerge from the world of choices the moment one person makes a suggestion, or takes a stance.

Principle of Sufficient Reason - This is not one of the three "classic" laws of thought, but many philosophers seem to agree that this ought to be included. The basic idea is that everything that exists (for example, your beliefs exist) has some reason for its existence. For the sake of these kinds of conversations we can apply this principle by saying that people always have reasons for what they believe. People's beliefs do not just magically spring into being. Maybe I believe certain facts about the world because that's how I was raised. Maybe I believe it because it makes the most sense to me. Maybe I changed my beliefs along the journey of my life because another set of beliefs provided a better explanation for the world. Or, maybe I changed my beliefs because I came to the conclusion that my previous beliefs "didn't work." Everybody's beliefs have a reason, and that's why we need to ask the important "why" questions. Once we understand the reasons then we can discuss whether the reasons are good reasons or not.

Other laws and principles have been proposed over the centuries which are also worth familiarizing yourself with, but these four have really surfaced as the cream of the crop, and I have found them to be foundational to successful dialogue.

As a quick aside, please don't get all legalistic about the application of these laws / principles in all conversations and in all circumstances. A certain amount of logical "grace" needs to be extended in all conversations. If somebody is not quite sure about why they believe something, don't start pouncing on them for violating the Principle of Sufficient Reason. Or, if somebody cannot provide a dictionary definition for some word they are using, or they are using the word slightly incorrectly (as long as it does not impact the thrust of the conversation), don't write up a ticket for breaking the Law of Identity.

Critical Thinking Spidey-Senses

I once saw a news headline that read, "Aliens coming in 25 years." Incredulous, I clicked on the link at Yahoo. The article was actually entitled, "Proof of Aliens Could Come Within 25 Years, Scientist Says."[9] Well, "proof of aliens" is a far cry from the aliens themselves, isn't it? Also, the use of the word, "could" is far more epistemologically humble than "Aliens coming." The original headline gave the impression that the aliens themselves were upon us; it's just a matter of time before we get to meet ET. But how many people, bombarded with dozens, maybe hundreds, of news stories in any given day will stop to ask how anybody could even possibly know the aliens' travel plans? Did the aliens send a postcard? How could we even know who these aliens are, or where they set out from? Even if we grant that most news readers are smart enough not to fall for that, how could the news writers have put such an obviously preposterous, and frankly misleading, news headline out there?

Like Spiderman who could sense that danger was imminent, even if he didn't know exactly what was upon him, another aspect of critical thinking that is truly foreign to a lot of people is the use of our "spidey senses" when it comes to what others are saying. Urban legends, internet hoaxes and scams

[9] **http://www.space.com/8958-proof-aliens-25-years-scientist.html** - If you read the article you should rightly ask how the Scientist can be so certain that the evidence will arrive on schedule. If we are unlikely to know the travel plans of aliens how much more unlikely are we to know the travel plans of the evidence for aliens?

are so popular and effective because people have not learned to judge something as "probably false" or "probably true" even if they don't know for certain, and cannot prove it. If you get an email from somebody in Nigeria claiming to offer you millions of dollars, your spidey-senses should start tingling. There may be no logical fallacies of any kind, but still, that just sounds wrong, doesn't it?

To help you hone your skills in doing a gut check on the likelihood that something is true or false, take time to skim through the Snopes website (see Bibliography). Remember, though, that just because something feels "probably" true or false does not guarantee it is.

You are what you read

As a last point, I want to highlight the importance of reading non-fiction and I don't mean self-help books. Read history, philosophy, science, political commentary, theology and so on. This may be the most effective means of training your mind to see, understand and analyze the claims of others. Read the works of those who see the world as you do, but make sure you also read the works of people on the other side of the fence. Through non-fiction you can learn how people formulate arguments, hopefully see some good examples in action, as well as broaden your mind in the process by learning new material. But remember, the purpose of reading non-fiction is not merely to learn facts, but also to **learn how to think**. As you read, keep asking yourself if the argument, as presented by the author, is good or bad. Even if you agree with it, challenge it. How would you improve it? You must develop a taste for these kinds of things, and that only comes with time and exposure.

And give up TV. I'm not kidding. Ideally just stop watching it except for rare occasions, but if that's not possible then cut back to as little TV time as you can handle. This will do many things for you. You will have the spare time you always complain that you lack. Frankly, TV is junk food for the brain (with very rare exceptions) and less junk food will help keep your brain in better shape. TV can suck the life out of family relationships. The list goes on. Give it a shot; you may just surprise yourself at the results.

Station 4 - What do I believe, and why?

Every belief / philosophy / religion needs to answer two fundamental questions, what is it and why believe it? These are obviously not the only two questions that can be asked about any particular worldview or philosophy, but these are the two bedrock questions that must be answered before any other answers are meaningful. These two questions are truly basic to any conversation where one person is trying to convince another person of something.

Suppose a salesman shows up at your door on a Saturday morning. What's the first thing they do? They introduce themselves and say who they are with. Right away they have begun answering the first question. Then, they explain a bit more about their product or service, continuing to answer the first question. Eventually they move on to tell you how wonderful their product is, and how easy they have made the payment plans, it has a great warranty, and so on. Now they are answering the second question.

Or, a political candidate knocks on your door. They tell you which party they represent (first question) and describe their qualifications and platform (second question). Or, your friend describes an all-inclusive resort in Cancun (first question) and shares stories of the fun they had (second question).

Just like these examples from every-day life, Christians need to answer these two most basic questions as well. Answers to these questions fall under the domains of Theology (What is it?) and Apologetics (Why believe it?).

What is it?

This question comes in various levels. First, what is the very broad, high-level, definition of Christianity? In other words, if we look at the common features of all Christian denominations, what separates them from the non-Christian beliefs? Then, we move into the specific beliefs you hold, like which denomination you belong to or what is your stance on various "in house" debates (age of the earth, end times, Catholicism / Protestantism, Calvinism /

Arminianism, etc). Not only is it important to understand what you believe, but you should also think through which of your beliefs are foundational to your worldview and which are more like icing on the cake. For instance, a believer in democracy would probably believe that a lack of coercion is foundational to a successful democracy, but they would probably not be as concerned with whether a nation elected their leader directly (USA) or indirectly (Canada). Christians tend to err in both directions on this count; some consider every last detail of their own theology vitally important, and others hardly take the time to consider Christian doctrine in the first place, implicitly stating that none of it is important. If you hold your Faith with any depth of sincerity then it is imperative that you understand the beliefs rather than simply parroting them.

There is a second challenge in this part; the ability to explain your beliefs to "outsiders." I work for an engineering company that does some pretty specialized analysis so one of the biggest challenges of my job is explaining the highly technical concepts to those who do not have a highly technical background. A big part of that process is translating specialized technical language into everyday language. Similarly, simply explaining Christianity in "Christian-ese" is a pointless enterprise if the person you are talking to has no idea what you are talking about. Learn to accurately describe your Faith in everyday language that non-Christians will be able to understand.

One of the unexpected perks of carefully working through your own beliefs is the fact that as your understanding improves, it will become evident in your life. Many people underestimate the spiritual growth that can occur as a result of the intellectual study of Theology. As the spiritual maturity becomes evident in your lives, questions will be asked and, conveniently enough, you will be better prepared to answer them!

Why believe it?

This is the second critical question. Understanding your beliefs gives you the ability to explain them to others, but the question will inevitably come up; why embrace those beliefs? There is a lot of competition out there these days; why choose your beliefs over the other guys?

There are two aspects to this question. First, why do YOU believe Christianity? What inspired YOU to choose Christianity over the other options? Here is where your testimony is invaluable; let people know what Jesus has done in your life. Take the time to work through your own testimony in such a way that you keep it down to three to five minutes. If your friend is interested in more than just the short version you can always take the time to spell out some of the details you glossed over, but don't initially bore them with a 30 minute version of your life story.

A second type of question emerges; is it reasonable for ANYBODY to believe that Christianity is true? In other words, you may believe in Jesus, but why should your friend believe in him too? Telling them about your testimony is not going to answer this question. You need to be prepared with some of the tools from phase 5 to address this question. Do NOT skip ahead; that time will come. In the mean time, focus on tweaking your testimony, and start reflecting on the most common challenges you have heard against the Christian Faith.

Station 5 - What do they believe, and why?

When you have conversations like these with people you get the privilege - and believe me when I say this is a deeply enjoyable part of the process - of learning about their beliefs. One of the greatest benefits of going through this part of the process is the wonder of better understanding your own perspective. It is ironic, but it works; trust me. More later.

Here are a few points to keep in mind during this part of the process:

- An individual may not hold to the official doctrines of the group. This happens within Christianity as well; quite often! Ask the person to explain their own beliefs rather than assuming that they tow the party line. You should, of course, familiarize yourself with the official doctrines as well and perhaps clarify where and why they diverge from them.

- When studying the doctrines of the group, get your information from their sources. To study Islam, read the Koran. To study Mormonism, read the Book of Mormon (and Doctrine and Covenants, and Pearl of Great Price). To understand Atheism, visit **www.infidels.org**. Many more resources are given in the resources section of this book.

- Also take the time to read Christian responses to their beliefs, but **only after learning their side of the story**. It will help you understand the points of greatest disagreement which serve as excellent starting points for discussion.

- Be very careful to gather accurate information. This cannot be overemphasized. The internet in particular is a wonderful blessing for society, but it can also serve to propagate a lot of false claims. Be very careful to ensure that you are getting accurate information. Clarify what you discover this with your friend. For instance, "I read such-and-such about your religion; is that correct?"

Phase 2 –Strategies for success

I have been doing something of an informal "experiment" when I have conversations of significance with people recently. I have begun by just talking with them and asking a lot of questions about them as people. What are you studying in University? What do you do for a living? That sounds like an interesting hobby, tell me more. Do you have pictures of your boat? Often times we get so far into their personal story that the philosophical differences that we were both expecting to discuss almost seem to get forgotten. This strategy has, so far, proven immensely beneficial. First, it benefits me. I get to learn some very interesting stuff because most people are surprisingly interesting. It has been personally rewarding just learning about subjects I would never, otherwise, learn about. It's like getting an education that you didn't have to pay for! Even if we don't end up discussing the important stuff for a long time (maybe never!) I just made a new friend, which is great in itself.

But there is a second reward. When the conversation turns to philosophical differences, we are now starting on friendly ground. We know each other. I have shown interest in them, and as we discuss the bigger issues of life they already know that I am not going to bite their head off. I'm a nice guy who cares, authentically, about their perspectives in life and about them as people. Notice, however, that the gracious conversation came after I made a personal connection with them. Notice, also (and perhaps more importantly) that the personal connection was not forced. I was not getting to know them just so I could check that off my list before we dove into the real meat of our discussion. I actually wanted to hear what they had to say. I actually found their life interesting. I was not faking it. If the conversation ended there that would have been perfectly acceptable. My interest is not for show or some kind of mere formality.

Before getting into any strategies, you need to understand that success in your actions begins with a successful perspective in your heart and mind. I will talk about treating other people kindly, focusing on Truth instead of personal glorification, and other such principles. But all of these actions and attitudes can be faked. I implore you not to fake them, but to take the much harder path of personal transformation. Invite Jesus to actually modify your heart and your mind so that you do not merely behave kindly toward others from a sense of duty, but that you bear in your heart a sincere, deep, desire for what is best for them, just like Jesus does![10] Ask Jesus to help you truly love the person who tells you that you are stupid for believing what you do. Allow Jesus to modify your thinking so that you sincerely yearn for Truth instead of just claiming to do so for the sake of appearing open-minded. Ask for guidance from the Holy Spirit to know which questions to ask about their life / career / hobbies so that you can really get to know them.

Did you imagine that preparing for conversations of significance with your non-Christian friends would require, and lead to, spiritual transformation in your own life? Expect it, pursue it and embrace it.

One other key point to always remember is this: whoever you are talking to is a person that has been carefully and lovingly crafted and sculpted by the Creator of the Universe. You are dealing with somebody about whom God cares very, VERY, deeply. If you harbor ungodly thoughts and attitudes toward them, consider that you might as well be pointing those thoughts and

---

[10] To be clear, I am not advocating the idea that love is about sentimentality. It's not like the Hollywood idea of warm-fuzzy feelings. You may not particularly want to be in the presence of that person, but you can still deeply love them. This is a hard concept to wrap your mind around, and even harder to live, but it is important when dealing with difficult people.

attitudes toward God himself. If you secretly hope they end up in Hell you might as well have nailed Jesus to the cross in person![11]

Station 6 - Very general strategies

The most general strategies relate directly to the first two stations we covered. First and foremost: **Leave your ego at home**. It's not about you, but about Truth. Never, EVER, forget this one. Humility is the order of the day.

Consider your state of mind before the conversation. Are you stressed? Are you tired? Perhaps you are still angry at what this person said to you last time you spoke. Maybe you need to postpone the conversation, or just keep a very close eye on your attitude, body language, tone of voice and so on.

Take notes. Preferably on paper, but that's not always possible.

- What are the primary discussion points?

- What are their specific claims / concerns?

- What evidence / reasons do they provide? Be specific.

- Are there any follow-up conversations or research you need to do?

Sometimes the conversation will come up unexpectedly, or perhaps you are talking over lunch when taking notes is difficult. In that case, you may want to jot down some thoughts in a "debriefing" document later that day. As soon as you have opportunity after the conversation, reflect on it. Answer the questions above, but also consider your own "performance." Were you able

---

[11] Matthew 5:21-22 is pretty clear on this point.. You will also notice that Matthew 5:43-44 does not read, "pretend to Love your enemy" or "make your enemy think you love them" but rather, we should bear in us an authentic love for all people.

to stay on topic? Did you handle yourself with gentleness and respect? Did you give the other person ample time to talk, or did you dominate the conversation? What would you do different? You cannot change the past, but the past can help you change for the better.

Be charitable with the other person. If they did not word something quite right, or their understanding of the facts is not exactly perfect, but their error does not impact their point, run with it. Don't major on the minors. Consider your friend who tries to convince you to vacation at a certain resort. If she made a great case for why you should go there, but she said it was only an hour or two to fly there and you know for certain that it's at least 4 hours; does that really matter? Now, if she got the price wrong, that would be significant! Let the little things slide, and give others the benefit of the doubt on trivial issues, when possible.

Pay careful attention to what your friend is saying verbally and non-verbally. Sometimes what we do not say is just as important as what we do say. If your friend is starting to become aggravated, maybe you need to back off a bit. If they keep trying to change the subject to something like the weather or television, maybe it's time to move on, for now. In some cases it may be appropriate to push them a little; if every time you bring up questions about the meaning of life they start talking about football then you might want to ask them why they seem to want to avoid that subject. Other times, though, it may be best to postpone the discussion. Also, if you notice that they start the conversation by claiming that Jesus does not exist, and it quickly moves to a conversation about their cousin who was abused by a priest, then discussions about Jesus' existence are probably not critical to them, just yet. Use discernment and be respectful. The more you honor their wishes (whether they state them or not) the more likely they are to keep the lines of communication open in the future because they will feel safe talking with you.

Don't shy away from making good points. For some people this is not a problem at all! For others (especially polite Canadians) this needs to be emphasized. Do not be afraid to challenge their perspectives right at the very core, but make sure you are careful how you challenge them. Consider these examples from a hypothetical conversation with a Muslim.

1) The Koran is a completely human invention, written by a demon-possessed pedophile.

2) From the parts of the Koran I've read, I don't see good reasons to think it is the word of God.

3) Tell me why you think the Koran is God's word.

The first is frankly offensive and unnecessarily so. Don't ever talk like that! The second and third are far more tactful, but you'll notice the subtle differences. The second is an assertion based on your own research, but even that assertion carries with it a note of humility; it remains open to the possibility that you are wrong. The last one is purely inquisitive with no claims being made at all, and yet your question cuts to the very heart of Islam; the real meat of the conversation. Never use the first approach, but which of the other approaches to use will depend on the context.

Acknowledge when they are right, or have a good point. Everybody has at least a little insight into Truth; you will never meet a person who is absolutely, always wrong in everything they say. It is important to highlight areas of truth and agreement for a couple of reasons. First, it reminds your friend that you are sincerely interested in Truth, rather than just trying to clobber them over the head. Second, sometimes those points of Truth and agreement can be used to establish other Truths in areas where you disagree.

Figure out what the key points are and stick with them. Suppose you describe the Biblical record of Jesus' claims about himself. Your friend doesn't even believe God exists because of evolution. You point out problems in the fossil record. Before you know it, you are discussing specific fossils that have been recovered in specific locations, and you are neck deep in discussions about whether this or that bone structure is more "fish like" or more "mammal like." Frankly, you've lost the point.

Similarly, figure out what the central problems are with the worldview of your friend and confront those instead of tangential issues. Here are some examples:

- Which is more central to Mormonism, that Joseph Smith engaged in polygamy or that the entire Christian Church for virtually all of the 2,000 years of its history was allegedly completely corrupted?

- Which is of greater relevance to Atheism; that certain fossils may or may not be transitional, or that we exist in a Universe that allows for life in the first place?

- Which is more devastating to moral relativism; that some moral relativist somewhere murdered people, or that virtually every moral relativist everywhere condemns them?

Walk past the mole hills; climb the mountains.

Find a Mentor. I always wish, looking back, that I would have had a mentor to help me learn to converse better with others. I had to learn most of these lessons myself - the very hard way, in fact - so unfortunately I only have very general advice to offer. Be on the lookout for somebody who has acquired more knowledge than you, knows how to handle that knowledge with grace and humility, is passionately interested in Truth instead of just getting along with everybody yet is pleasant to converse with, even when you disagree. That sounds a lot like a description of Christ himself, so it wouldn't hurt if they were further along their spiritual journey than you are.

Station 7 - More specific strategies

Start with asking questions. [12] This will seem a little strange to some people, but I firmly believe this is the best way to approach these kinds of

[12] I've read several influential thinkers on how Christianity can best engage the culture and they seem to agree; lots of questions and epistemic humility are highly effective.

conversations. How can that be, considering we are trying to point them toward the Truth? If we ask them questions, that means we are gathering information from them; information we believe is wrong. How is that helping either of us move toward the Truth?

Here are several reasons to start with asking questions.

- What if they are right? Wouldn't you want to know that you were wrong? If you are sincerely entering the conversation as a pursuit of Truth then you need to be open to the prospect that your views are wrong and their views are right. Scary? It should be, but consider this; if you sincerely believe that you are right then wouldn't you want them to listen with an open mind? If you want them to, why wouldn't you do the same for them?

- Questions show that you are legitimately interested in understanding their perspective. Make sure your question-asking is authentic. If you are just asking questions because some guy in some book said you should and you really cannot wait to get to the part where you tell them about Jesus, they will know that you are being deceptive.

- Understanding their perspective helps you figure out how to present the Gospel. Muslims need to hear it differently than Buddhists.

- Questions can be a non-aggressive means to help them see flaws in their own perspectives.[13]

I cannot over-emphasize the importance of the last point. I recall a conversation I had with a couple of Atheists about the "Genocide Awareness Project" that a pro-life group of University students put on. The posters showed graphic images of aborted babies. These Atheists claimed that such a tactic was just wrong. In fact, they were rather adamant about it, and said so

[13] This video is a wonderful, and VERY brief, illustration of this general principle - **http://youtu.be/qySx8tSs8BQ**

repeatedly. I politely asked them, "Why? What makes it wrong?" They fumbled about for an answer for a minute or two and finally started pondering between them whether such a strategy would really change anybody's mind anyway. I clarified that something can be ineffective (the essence of their answer) without being wrong, so I was still curious why they thought it was wrong, rather than merely ineffective. They fumbled around for an answer again and eventually focused on the fact that the group who was doing these protests allegedly received funding from foreign lobby groups. I was fairly certain this University club was connected with a Canadian organization, which I pointed out, but I then asked them why it was wrong that they got foreign funding, if that was truly the case. More fumbling, more diversion, and eventually I let the conversation go because I just met these folks and did not want to focus too much on the fact that their bold proclamations had not been well reasoned or researched.

Indeed, in many ways this is probably the single most effective strategy you can use to help somebody see the error in their own beliefs, and here's why. If you simply **tell** your friend that their beliefs are wrong, or that their beliefs are self-refuting, they will not typically like to hear that, nor will they open their mind to what you are saying. However, when you **ask** them to explain their views, and specifically you ask about the apparent contradiction in their views, then their mind cannot avoid the inconsistency. The question forces them to face the problems, but you are not the bad guy because you did not force it on them; you simply asked perfectly natural questions.

People's beliefs are usually a combination of truth and error. And I do mean all people; both Christians and non-Christians! But if everybody believes at least some truth, then the aspects of your friends beliefs that are true almost certainly overlap your true beliefs as well. Starting on common ground, you can use questions to move them toward those parts of their beliefs that are false. True beliefs will usually contradict false beliefs, so you can ask questions that help reveal the internal contradiction. Again, I strongly recommend Greg Koukl's book, *Tactics*, to further explain this absolutely invaluable tool for discussions.

Lastly, I want to re-emphasize what I mentioned previously; gaining a better understanding of somebody else's beliefs helps you better understand, and gain a new appreciation for, Christianity and God. This is perhaps the most surprising benefit of asking questions. James A. Beverley describes a dinner he had with the high priest of the Church of Satan, "the interchange with [Peter H.] Gilmore and a new examination of Satanism increased my appreciation for the Gospel."[14] He provides several concrete examples by way of comparison, and the juxtaposition of the two belief systems shed new light on a Faith he almost certainly knows better than most Christians.

Do not fear an open mind, just bring along your critical thinking skills.

Focus on the two key lines of questions. Remember from Station 4 that there are two fundamental questions that every worldview must answer. Make sure that many / most of your questions fall into these two categories or at least guide the conversation in these two directions.

- **What do you believe?** Get them to explain their beliefs in sufficient detail. Ask clarifying questions.

- **Why do you believe it?** What is their evidence / reason?

Many people are not prepared to answer the "why" questions. It is not uncommon for people to accept some things in life that they have not deeply analyzed. You probably have; I know I have. Don't pounce on them or belittle them. Be gentle, but assertive when you point out that they have not questioned their own beliefs. And, of course, make sure that you are prepared to answer the "why" questions about your own beliefs.

To have doubted one's own first principles is the mark of a civilized man.
Oliver Wendell Holmes, Jr.

---

[14] Dinner with the High Priest is in the May/June 2012 issue of Faith Today (page 45), a magazine put out by the Evangelical Fellowship of Canada. James A. Beverley is professor of Christian thought and ethics at Tyndale Seminary. If somebody with his credentials has something to learn from other beliefs, I humbly suggest we all do!

None of their questions / topics are off limits. They will have challenges & questions to your own beliefs; take them seriously! When they ask why God killed their mother with cancer, don't brush off the question. When they demand an explanation for why God instructed the Israelites to slaughter infants in Canaan, don't avoid the issue. If they throw the Crusades at you, don't get defensive. If they wonder why so many televangelists run off with their secretaries don't sidestep the question. If you avoid certain subjects, it gives the impression that you have something to hide. Here are some general strategies.

- Many times you will not have an immediate answer; don't worry. The biggest mistake you can make is to fake an answer. If you get caught making it up (and you will eventually get caught) that stains everything else you've said. Rather than fake an answer, try saying something like, "That's a good question, let me write it down and get back to you later." Don't forget to follow up their question! If you simply cannot find a good answer, admit it. People are often far more understanding than we think, and are more likely to respect somebody who admits humility than somebody who fakes confidence.

- When you get into subjects that you simply don't understand, admit it! If they object to the need for God as an explanation for the universe because the law of gravity can explain the origin of our universe (it can't, but that's a subject for another day), if you don't understand what they are talking about, just admit it. If they are not willing to recognize that you are merely human then that's their problem. However, there may be some subjects that you need to pro-actively familiarize yourself with if they are very important to your friend. If it's beyond you, find another Christian who understands what they're talking about and can help you out, or is willing to talk with your friend.

- Help them see that some questions, though fair game, are not ultimately relevant. Sometimes they will deliberately drag you down pointless rabbit trails; don't be afraid to call them on that (politely, of course). For instance, if you end up spending exorbitant amounts of time discussing the fact that some political candidate somewhere who claims to be a Christian made some comment that they find personally offensive, that's probably not really a fruitful discussion to spend a lot of time on. Address it as best you can and move on.

You can only control your own behavior, so DO IT. Some people (even friends) will turn the conversation quite negative. Do not be surprised when people do this; we are all human. You cannot control them, but you can, and must, control yourself.

- NEVER get angry, hostile, etc. They may not return the favor, but that's their choice, not yours. Of course, don't give them reason to get angry either!

- Never attack them. Never tell them they're going to hell for their beliefs. Never belittle them or their views (i.e. "you'd have to be pretty stupid…")

- When they commit logical fallacies, or make some claim that is demonstrably false, point that out politely and move on instead of taking on a "gotcha" attitude.

- Learn when (and how) to diplomatically end a conversation even if it gives the impression that you "lost." Remember, it's not about you winning or losing.

No matter what they say, or how they behave, always make sure you can stand before your Lord at the end of the conversation confident that he is thinking, "well done, good and faithful servant."

Talk in person. This one cannot be overstated. The use of the internet as a means for people to connect has been an immense blessing for society, on the whole, but there are some very serious downsides to using it as a means for discussing matters of significance. Whenever possible, meet people over coffee, dinner, playing sports, going for a hike or anything else where you are in their physical presence, talking face to face. Perhaps the only exception to this rule might be Skype or some other such technology. Facebook, email and discussion forums are recipes for disaster, and here are some reasons why:

- Like it or not, our present generation has lost a LOT of the fine art of writing with clarity. Thus, whatever you wrote will probably not exactly reflect what you were thinking. It is a frequent source of misunderstanding that is best avoided when you talk in person, giving you and your friend the opportunity to clarify things on the fly.

- Thanks to Postmodernism (much more later) many people are in the habit of ignoring what an author meant, and finding "my own" meaning to what they read. In other words, even if you worded it perfectly to exactly convey what you were trying to say, it will quite frequently be twisted and re-interpreted according to somebody else's perspective. It is much harder to do this in person when you can immediately correct them.

- What exists in electronic form exists FOREVER. Even a single mistake can haunt you for the rest of your life!

- Electronic communication (excluding video discussion, to some extent) lacks the non-verbal which is often critical in understanding what a person really means. For instance, many people will instinctively use sarcasm and forget that it does not work so well in written text form, even with the politely smiley at the end. :-)

- Lastly, and this is perhaps most important, there is this bizarre tendency for the nicest people to take on an alter ego when they are in discussion forums or exchanging emails. Things you would never say to a person's face are suddenly fair game when you are behind the "safety" of your laptop. I've done it. I've seen other Christians do it. I most certainly have seen non-Christians do it. It is most easily avoided if you resolve that the most important conversations in life take place in the "danger" of a coffee house.

Having said all that, please don't make it a rule to never use the internet for conversations of significance; some Christians are even called specifically to internet ministry. There is a time and a place for that, but be very careful to make sure it is the right time and place, and to make sure that what you write very clearly conveys what you mean to say. Also, you will need to be extra gracious with the other person; interpreting what they write in the most positive light possible, and quickly forgiving them if they attack you in any way as people sometimes will.

There is a time to speak and a time to remain silent. This is a hard one to deal with because people will tend to either want to talk all the time on every subject, or to zip it whenever something controversial comes up. There are no solid rules about when to talk and when to keep silent, but consider which of the two impulses you gravitate toward. Trust God to guide you on these ones, and listen carefully to the prompting of his Spirit.

Consider this; Jesus' clearest declarations of his Messianic identity were given only to certain people at certain times. Even that history-transforming Truth was not revealed everywhere, at all times, and to all people, equally.

Be all things to all people.[15] Bear in mind your audience. Some people will respond better to a soft conversation where you gently exchange ideas and other people may connect better with somebody who lays it all on the line and powerfully asserts their viewpoint. In discussions with other Apologists we have observed that most Atheists interpret the dove-like approach as a sign of intellectual weakness; it actually turns them off further from Jesus. Discussions with them should probably be somewhat more "frontal assault" in nature, but obviously with the respect and civility that is always required. That approach, however, will probably rarely work on somebody who is neck-deep in New Age "positivistic" thinking. Some people may respond best to straight-forward, linear presentation of ideas while others may better understand through parables and illustrations. In fact, given Jesus' preference for the latter style of teaching I suspect the that method is more universally effective.

[15] This is similar to the concept described in 1 Corinthians 9:19-23

The flip side of this, however, is that you are built a certain way and you may not be skilled in the "right" kind of conversation with certain people. This is rarely a show-stopper, actually, but sometimes you may need to acknowledge your own limitations (even to them!) and introduce them to somebody else who may be more suitably built to handle their kind of discussion. Perhaps you need to develop your skills in other areas.

Phase 3 – Learn from the mistakes of others

We can all learn from our mistakes, but it is much better to learn from the mistakes of others so we can improve ourselves without having to experience the bumps and bruises that typical accompany those errors.

Station 8 - General mistakes

The most common mistakes are basically forgetting the rules mentioned previously, so I'll just go over them quickly.

Getting angry or hostile. I have seen people attack with an attitude of condescension and a "greater than thou" mentality. I've been told my IQ is less than that of a potted plant. This is probably the most common mistake people make so be ready for it. They may do this with you, but make sure you never return "eye for eye."

Making it about being right (ego-driven) rather than discovering Truth (Truth-driven). Making it about proving your intellectual/spiritual superiority.

Talking more than listening. You should strive to ask questions more often than you provide answers. Francis Schaeffer said that if he knew he only had 60 minutes with a person he would spend the first 55 of those minutes asking questions.

Forgetting to use three simple and highly effective words, "**I don't know**." Humility will get you miles further than a facade of knowledge.

No matter what your friend says/does, never duplicate their mistakes. If they insult, never let it upset you. If they raise the volume, you drop it down a notch. If worse comes to worse, "let's pick this up another time."

Station 9 - Common fallacies

In Phase 4 I discuss Postmodernism in greater depth, but for now I will simply highlight that one of the effects of Postmodernism on our society is a reduced respect for the use of Reason as a means to discover Truth. When people stopped caring about Reason, they stopped using it properly. As a result, people regularly make all kinds of logical mistakes when they talk to each other. As mentioned previously, these are called fallacies. There are dozens, maybe hundreds, of different kinds of fallacies people can make, so I'll just cover some of the more common ones here. Again, "A Rulebook for Arguments" is a strongly recommended resource for this subject.

Straw Man. This is simply the mistake of misrepresenting somebody else's view so that you can "disprove" it. An example of this might be the claim that Christianity is about three gods being one god and that's illogical. Well, yes, that is illogical, but that is not what Christianity teaches. If somebody refutes this claim, then they have not refuted Christianity but a "straw man" imitation of Christianity.

Some Christians mistakenly think that Atheists are somehow "anti-morals" which is quite obviously not the case. Other people will misrepresent your views; do not misrepresent theirs. Also, be gracious when you correct them.

Ad Hominem. This fallacy essentially means some claim must be false because there is something wrong with the person making the claim. A simple example might be that Christianity must be false because Christians are such bad people.

This is not to be confused with simply insulting a person which is not so much a fallacy as it is just bad taste. You should avoid that too, obviously. Avoid it, but also expect it from some people!

Red Herring. When somebody throws in some utterly irrelevant point this is what a Red Herring is all about. Suppose somebody were to say, "Christianity cannot be true. Besides, you guys oppose alcohol." Ignore the fact that most Christians do not oppose alcohol at all, even if they did, that has absolutely nothing to do with whether or not Christianity is true.

Genetic Fallacy. This fallacy asserts that something cannot be trusted because of where it came from (i.e. it's "genetics"). One very common example is the claim that we cannot trust the New Testament because it was written by Christians, who were biased. Or suppose a political activist fought some proposed government legislation because it was originally conjured up by "Big Oil." By the same thinking, we cannot trust Muslims to describe Islam, Atheists to describe Atheism or Buddhists to describe Buddhism. We definitely cannot trust environmentalists to explain the state of affairs with respect to the environment, can we?

Equivocation. This simply means twisting the meaning of words. One of the most common examples of this that I have seen relates to discussions about the origin of the Universe. Atheists often describe the fact that science has observed that virtual particles come into being out of "nothing" and therefore, it is possible for the entire Universe to come into being out of "nothing" without God's participation. The problem resides in their definition of the word "nothing," which you would think is a pretty self-explanatory word.[16] They are using a very specific definition of the word describing a very specific scientific concept related to the Quantum Vacuum, whereas most people mean it in the common usage sense - a lack of any thing at all, even Quantum Vacuum Energy.

---

[16] Edward Feser does his usual magnificent job of dissecting this confusion with a dash of wit and a large dose of reasonable analysis.
http://edwardfeser.blogspot.com/2011/11/what-part-of-nothing-dont-you.html

Station 10 - Common rhetorical tactics

Along with the increased use of fallacious reasoning, people these days are also far more prone to use certain rhetorical tactics that give the false impression of "victory" without actually moving anybody closer to the Truth.

False facts. This one is stunningly common. Many people will confidently assert some fact about reality that is completely and utterly false. One of my favorites (because I have even seen scholars make this mistake) is the claim that everybody used to think the earth was flat until Columbus prove otherwise. Do the research, this claim is one big hoax that has been perpetuated for centuries.[17] Since even before the time of Christ the common consensus (at least among the educated) was that the earth is spherical. This is true across all the major world civilizations, as far as I understand.

Everyone is entitled to his own opinions, but not his own facts.
Daniel Patrick Moynihan

Incidentally, the best way to test for false facts is to ask your friend for proof. This is a perfectly fair question, but one they will not be able to answer unless their facts are true. It's also a lot more polite than accusing them of lying! Remember, questions first. For instance:

"Europeans at the time of Columbus used to believe the earth was flat"
"Can you list some names of medieval scholars who believed that?"

"Science has disproven God."
"Really? I am interested in that! Could you show me which scientists were involved in that study? Which scientific journal was it published in? What was their methodology?"

Conversely, some false facts involve a LACK of some kind of evidence. What you need to do is show them that such evidence actually does exist.

[17] **http://en.wikipedia.org/wiki/Myth_of_the_Flat_Earth**

"The divinity of Christ was invented at the Council of Nicea. Nobody believed Jesus was divine before that."

"That's interesting. How do you explain the early church fathers who regularly claimed that Jesus was God, even a century prior to Nicea? Are you familiar with the Meggido Inscription in an early church building that dedicates the church 'to God Jesus Christ?' That church building was constructed prior to the Council of Nicea."

A closely related rhetorical tactic is misleading facts. In this case the facts are technically true, but upon further investigation you find that some very important contextual information has been left out that sheds a whole new light on the significance of the facts. A popular example of this is the claim that there are more textual variants within the New Testament manuscripts that have survived from antiquity (perhaps as high as 500,000 variants) than there are words in the New Testament itself (just fewer than 140,000). Technically, that is true, but the larger picture is deliberately left out. We have so many variants precisely because we have so many manuscript copies; almost 6,000, in fact. If we average the variants across all those manuscripts you would end up with fewer than 100 variants per manuscript, or about 1 variant per 1,400 words. That is an entirely different picture, isn't it?[18]

Larger than life claims. One of the most common examples of this is "science has proven..." This could also include other such claims like "all scholars believe" or "we all know" and so on. Basically people like to make it seem overwhelmingly obvious that their perspective is correct so they won't have to actually defend it. Now, if science has actually proven something, or all (or nearly all) scholars actually do believe something then you should at least take it seriously instead of just dismissing it. But before you believe your friend, confirm their claims; don't just assume they are either right or wrong.

One of the most common larger than life claims that I hear over and over again is the claim that there is "no evidence for God." Notice that they are not saying there is no **good** evidence, nor are they saying that the evidence

[18] For a much more thorough explanation of this particular issue, I highly recommend the free iTunesU course *The Basics of New Testament Textual Criticism* made available through the *Center for the Study of New Testament Manuscripts*.

dose not convince them, they are claiming that there actually is not any evidence for God of any sort to be found anywhere! Phase 5 will provide some resources to counter this obviously hyperbolic claim.

Shock and Awe. Sometimes this involves fast-talking like a used car salesman, and other times it is as simple as piling your plate so high with claims and allegations that it would take you weeks to sort through it all and respond to each one. This will often take the form of "drive by philosophy" such as the very common, "Jesus, **if he even existed**, said..." Notice how they can include the subtle claim that perhaps Jesus never even existed without offering any defense of the claim. By adding four little words they have a leg up in the conversation because they have planted doubt, whereas it might take you some time to even begin to unravel that common allegation. If they pack a few short sentences with a large number of "drive by philosophy" claims then you'll end up chasing your tail for the rest of your chat.[19] Get them to pick one subject and stick with it; that's not an unreasonable request.

Demonize the other guy. I had a Facebook chat with somebody once about homosexuality where I pointed out that there are certain myths that society has perpetuated about homosexuality that are simply false. They replied that it was awful of me to interfere with people's lives, and if I hated freedom so much I should move to Saudi Arabia. Notice that I never said anything about interfering in anybody's life, nor did I say anything about freedom. I simply pointed out that many people believe certain claims about Homosexuality that clinical studies have shown to be false.[20] They were simply not prepared to show that the myths were actually facts (remember what I said about "false facts"), so they were attempting to silence me by making me look like the "bad guy." This is an intimidation tactic and nothing more. If they can make you FEEL bad for believing what you believe (even if they have to misrepresent you in the process - Straw Man) then they avoid the hard work of disproving your beliefs because they expect you to keep quiet.

---

[19] In a debate where his opponent stocked up a huge pile of claims, Dinesh D'Souza responded, "I feel like a mosquito at a nudist colony; I am trying to decide where to begin." Cute, and it makes the point! - **http://youtu.be/PSeHsCPayXM**

[20] I made reference to the wealth of resources available at **http://www.NARTH.com**.

Making mountains out of molehills. Sometimes the details matter, and sometimes they do not. Some people enjoy picking apart absolutely everything you say to find the slightest discrepancy so they can parade it around as though it represents a thorough refutation of your entire worldview. Suppose you are talking about the prevalence of Trinitarian theology in the pre-Nicean Church and you mistakenly claim that the Council of Nicea occurred in AD 350. Now, the Council was actually 25 years prior to that, but does the date make one iota of difference to that particular discussion? It might make a difference if you claimed it was in 125 AD, or in 1325 AD, but that little error is well worth correcting and moving on. If your friend turns that into the focus of the discussion then they are using some bad rhetorical tactics to avoid the real subject.

You are always, always, wrong. Sometimes you will be in conversation with somebody who will attempt to refute absolutely everything you say on every subject, no matter what your perspective, down to the smallest detail. This is particularly common in email exchanges where a person will take your original email which may have been just a couple of paragraphs, and turn it into a multi-page treatise on how wrong you are about everything you wrote in virtually every sentence. This is obviously similar to the "shock and awe" tactic whereby they pile on more and more "problems" for you to deal with until you are drowning. It serves no helpful purpose in the pursuit of Truth but instead gives the false impression that they have "thoroughly" refuted your views. It is painful, but if you take the time to sift through the pile you will often find that they spend more time on irrelevant subjects and less time on the core of your argument.

Many other examples of fallacies and rhetorical tactics are often used; familiarize yourself with them and don't make those mistakes. During conversations keep an eye on what your friend is saying and ask yourself if this feels like some other kind of rhetorical tactic that you have not heard of yet. With time you will learn to separate reasoned conversation from mere rhetoric.

Station 11 - Mistakes Christians make

Christians are prone to making all the same mistakes as those listed above, but there are also a handful of mistakes that are rather unique to Christians.

Let me share my testimony. Often times when non-Christians raise some objection to Christianity, we instinctively respond with our testimony. We seem to think that if we tell them about the deep personal impact that Jesus has had in our own lives, then their intellectual concerns will miraculously vanish. This is a very misguided instinct. Stick to the topic and if you are ill-equipped to address thc topic then admit as much, go home and do your homework. There is a time and a place for you to tell your friend what God has done in your life, but sometimes our testimony is relied on too heavily when it simply is not appropriate to the context of the conversation.

Another similar mistake is to rely too heavily on the Bible. Think about it; if your friend already trusted the Bible then they would probably already be a Christian. At the end of the day we need to point people toward God, as revealed in the Bible, so we obviously need to eventually end up there, but there are many instances where we need to think outside the Bible first. Part of your job will be to help them understand **why we trust the Bible** before they will seriously consider what it has to say.[21]

I want you to consider Christianity, but I don't want to hear about your beliefs. Too many Christians (especially those who **really** love evangelism) want to "cut to the chase" and tell their friends (or complete strangers) about Jesus. This passion is good, in one sense, but can be taken to an unhealthy extreme. If you seriously want people to openly consider Jesus, why are you unwilling to listen to their beliefs? They see this double standard and are turned off by it, and rightly so! I would go so far as to say that

[21] Elsewhere I describe how I believe we need to start outside Christianity and the Bible and move in from there. Others disagree, and they would disagree with this point as well. To understand their views, familiarize yourself with something called Presuppositional Apologetics. I do not adhere to that perspective, but there are smart, dedicated Christian scholars who do. I could be wrong; educate yourself.

Christians should not bother sharing the Gospel with others unless they are willing to first seriously learn about what that other person believes.

I cannot explain the "what" and "why" of Christianity. Can you explain how the Bible points to the Trinitarian Doctrine? Are you familiar with the claim that the Bible is corrupt? How do you respond? Can you provide and defend just one of the lines of evidence for God's existence? If all you do is tell people about Jesus, but cannot answer even the most basic questions they ask, that reveals that you haven't really given it serious thought.[22] This helps further the "check your brains at the door" perspective that many people have about Christianity.

Interestingly, one of the things a lot of Christians find most difficult is simply explaining what Christianity is all about. More specifically, can you explain it without using phrases like "substitutionary atonement" and "the blood of Jesus paid our debts?" Specific terms explaining Christian Theology are important, but you need to bring the concepts down to the level of the average person on the street. Speak in a language they will understand. As I mentioned earlier, you need to be able to explain Christianity in "normal" language instead of Christian-ese.

Conversion in the next five minutes. You've probably heard of Romans Road, and seen those tracts that some people hand out. Sometimes that is useful, so don't knock it, but most of the time they simply fall on deaf ears because the goal seems to be instant conversion. If you only have limited time in the discussion (stranger on an airplane trip, etc), point them in the right direction, but don't force the end game. God will work elsewhere. Maybe leave your email address with them so you can connect over coffee later.

If you have plenty of time (i.e. co-worker, neighbor, etc), take it slowly and in multiple sittings. You are probably in this for the long haul. Expect to invest years in the process, and it will not always succeed.

---

[22] At the website **http://johnlennox.org** watch the video "The Christian Use of Mind." This is an excellent, and brief, commentary on the subject.

It's all me, or it's all God. Some Christians forget that God expects us to be involved in people's conversion so they think all they need to do is pray and make their lives a witness to their non-Christian friends. Wrong; you need to actually engage others on a spiritual / worldview level. God expects you to move far beyond just mowing their lawn and bringing them pies on occasion. Many Christians have this misconception that Faith is not, fundamentally, an intellectual exercise, but a spiritual one. It is both. Much more could be said - especially since some Christians have gone out of their way to quote-mine the Bible into proving their "ant-intellectual" perspective - so I'll just leave the subject here and recommend that you read the book "Love your God with all your Mind" by J P Moreland. Pray, absolutely, but just remember that God is only taking on half of the job; he was quite serious about the Great Commission.

Other Christians forget that God ultimately draws people to himself so they get an over-inflated perception of their role in the process. The weight of your friend's afterlife should not rest on your shoulders. Dialogue with them, take their questions and objections seriously, pray for them, befriend them at all times and entrust everything to God.

Your resistance is rooted in SIN. There is, obviously, an element of truth to this because the foundational root of rebellion against God is the appeal of sin. However, to dismiss their challenges, objections and questions as though they are just a cover for their sinful desires is a bad idea. There are some for whom "the creed follows the deed," in that their worldview is used to justify lifestyle preferences that are inconsistent with the Bible, but for others the questions and challenges are quite sincere and they are open to good answers. There are many, many, stories of converts to Christ who only came to Christ after somebody took their questions seriously.

The flip side of this is that there are many, many, stories of ex-Christians who have left the faith in part because their questions were either ignored or actively denounced. Their questions were not sinful, but the response of the Church to their questions most certainly was.

Phase 4 - Successful Failures

Failure is inevitable. I don't want to give the wrong impression that these, or any other strategies for friendly arguments, will always result in happy endings. This isn't a Disney fairy tale. Let's face it; even Jesus, during his earthly ministry, was unable to persuade everybody of the Truth, and if God cannot persuade every human of the Truth, what makes you think you can? There will be times when, no matter how well you behave yourself, or how effectively you utilize the skills you learn in this book (and others) you may still lose friends or end conversations in stalemate.

We can thank Postmodernism for much of this, today.[23] If you don't know much about Postmodernism then you need to educate yourself because Western Civilization is drowning in it at all levels, and suffering the consequences. You have almost certainly had your thinking impacted by it to some extent. Two of the key ideas of Postmodernism that relate to this subject are:

---

[23] The Stanford Encyclopaedia of Philosophy summarizes, "that postmodernism is indefinable is a truism." (**http://plato.stanford.edu/entries/postmodernism/**) I am not concerned with the academic version of Postmodernism articulated and defended by professional philosophers, but rather with the folk-level version that has permeated our society. Dr. Groothuis (Apologetics Survey, lecture 4, around 1:07:00) refers to Postmodernism as "a social atmosphere" that is not so much arrived at after serious contemplation, as it is just accepted in vague terms by a broad cross-section of our culture. You'll find it in the Church too!

1. You make your own Truth; nobody's Truth is more right than anybody else's.

2. Truth is discovered by looking inside myself. Reason is a tool for manipulation, not for discovering the Truth.

The first one has been particularly heavily applied to the question of ethics, morality, religion and social justice issues. Those who have been consumed by Postmodern thinking - and that's a lot of people - are particularly likely to say things like, "if that works for you, then it is right for you," or "don't impose your views on me." The underlying idea is that reality (even moral law) is customizable; we tailor it for ourselves. To suggest that some facts or rules apply to everybody regardless of whether we like them or not goes completely against Postmodern thinking. William Lane Craig is a leading Christian Philosopher and Apologist with many years of experience presenting and debating the veracity of the Christian Faith in various academic settings. In his experience the biggest challenge that Christians face when presenting their Faith is the challenge of relativism. "[Students] think that religious beliefs are mere expressions of personal taste or opinion. As a result, when Christians claim that they know the truth about these matters, people are deeply offended and think of Christians as bigoted, dogmatic, and even immoral people."[24] It has nothing to do with whether Christianity is true or not and everything to do with the idea that any worldview is right versus any other worldview. The idea that nothing can be said to be "right" or "wrong" in any kind of objective sense is clearly the fruit of Postmodernism.

This complicates matters with respect to discussing issues, such as moral issues, with Postmoderns. You would think that we could have a good healthy discussion about the facts and the analysis of the facts, but that does not typically work with Postmoderns because the very use of Reason is not considered trustworthy, as mentioned in the second point. The idea that you should investigate the facts, understand how logic works, learn how to avoid fallacies - basically everything I've described up to this point - is seen as useless because they do not believe that's how you arrive at truth. Facts

[24] **http://www.reasonablefaith.org/a-few-minutes-with-dr-william-lane-craig-interview-by-john-d-martin**

become "your facts." Truth becomes "your truth." The first point was that there are no absolutes, therefore in the Postmodern mind there is no absolute Truth to be discovered in the first place. Hence, Reason and Logic are useless tools because "truth" is whatever they feel like, whatever works for them, whatever they create for themselves. It need not reflect reality.

How does this play out? If I try to convince somebody that they are mistaken, what I am doing is trying to show that their perception of reality does not line up with reality itself. For the Postmodern, though, there is no external reality to be aligned with in the first place. To the Postmodern mind claiming that they are mistaken is an attack on the "truth" that they have within them. Frankly, from their perspective, I am attacking them personally![25] One of the first criticisms you are likely to hear, as Dr. Craig suggested, is that you are being offensive or inappropriate. When you claim that their beliefs may need to be reconsidered, **what you are doing** is making a claim about their beliefs, not about them. **What they hear** is a criticism about themselves because beliefs are almost put on par with skin color, gender, and other such components of personal identity. Is it any wonder so many relationships fail these days?[26]

I do not want to give the impression that Postmodernism is pure evil, or that every facet of it should be rejected out of hand. Furthermore, Postmodernism is hardly the only cause of people rejecting the truth, though it often exacerbates other causes. Despite its major faults (and they are truly foundational, not merely peripheral) there are certain aspects of Postmodernism that are praiseworthy. Postmodernism began as a response to the Modernist movement (hence the name) and in many ways it tried to correct the errors and excesses of Modernity; those corrections were well-

---

[25] Dr. Groothuis does a lot of public speaking, including Q&A sessions. From his experience, "we so identify people with their beliefs that if we disagree with their beliefs it is a hate crime." (Apologetics Survey, lecture 7, 15:00)

[26] Based on the description I have given here, many people may think of Postmoderns as some strange group of people they have never met. It is far more prevalent than most people recognize, and almost everybody in Western Societies (probably even you!) has had their thinking at least somewhat influenced by this philosophy. Know Thyself.

intentioned and certainly necessary. Postmodernism also emphasizes people's individuality, and this focus on the uniqueness of every person is something that Christians ought to keep in mind! Rather than trying to fit everybody into cookie-cutter molds, Postmodernism celebrates you, whoever you are. I have seen all too many Christian churches that quite obviously appeal only to successful upper-middle class people who fit, seamlessly, into a "normal" society. We could definitely use a little rocking of the boat with widely divergent personality types and people who do not "fit;" the kind of people Jesus spent most of his time with.

However, while we learn from its strengths, we must recall that Postmodernism's weaknesses are major, they are foundational, and they have had catastrophic effects on our culture and our relationships. Embrace the wheat, throw out the chaff.

So, due to the negative impact Postmodernism has had on society - and because of various other reasons people choose to reject Truth - you are stuck with a dilemma, just like I described at the beginning of this book. You can either choose to remain silent while they boldly proclaim their perspective, so that you can maintain your friendship, or you can shine a light on a different perspective and lose a friend simply because you think differently than they do and will not remain silent. Sometimes friendships will fail because you chose to exercise the same freedom of speech that your friend obviously enjoys and it does not matter how diplomatic you are.

So failure is sometimes inevitable, even if you do absolutely everything right. Of course, you will not always do everything right, and even those failures are good for something. Let's explore a slightly more detailed definition of "success" than the one I provided at the beginning of the book.[27]

Level 1 Success - You maintain your composure during the conversation. Your friend does not.

---

[27] I should probably include another, more fundamental, level of success; that you have a conversation at all. It is not uncommon to find people unwilling to discuss anything of significance. I call this "Apathism" and its prevalence is ever-increasing.

Level 2 Success - You and your friend both maintain your composure during the conversation. Nobody changes their mind.

Level 3 Success - You and your friend both maintain your composure during the conversation, and one of you is corrected from their error (hint, it may be you!).

If Level 3 success occurs then congratulations, that's the best form of success you can possibly have. Frankly, though, that is rare and little commentary is necessary, so let's look at the other levels.

Station 12 - Pleasant, but "ineffective," conversations

Suppose you only get to Level 2 success. In this situation you have pleasant, respectful, conversation in which you disagree with each other at the beginning, and you still disagree at the end. What benefit is there to having these conversations? There are many benefits!

- You have planted seeds of Truth that may come to fruition one day. For many people conversion does not happen overnight, or with a single friend. It can take years and involves many people. You may never see the results of your gentle persuasion.

- You get a chance to practice the art of logic, reason, and building a case via argumentation. This skill is best honed in the real world where you try, fail, and fall flat on your face. Pleasant conversations are the best place to practice these skills.

- You and your friend both grow slightly more accustomed to respectful dialogue. The more that people can get used to this, perhaps the more that people will come to expect it instead of the verbal violence we see all too often. It lays the groundwork for an open, trusting, relationship for years to come.

- Perhaps others were watching, and perhaps they are not used to seeing Christians behave themselves. There are some bad examples of Christians out there (I definitely used to be one of them), so the more we can show that not all Christians are like that, the more positively we present Jesus to others.

It would seem inevitable that a person would accept the Truth if they merely understood it and saw the good reasons for accepting it. Why do people still avoid the Truth? Making a worldview shift is no small matter. Just imagine how difficult it would be if somebody proved to you, beyond a shadow of a doubt, that Jesus was a fraud and not the Son of God. Would you enthusiastically embrace the Truth? I know I would be very reluctant because I have a lot invested in Christianity. Similarly, many people will resist accepting Christ in part because they do not want it to be true[28] and also in part because Christianity has a rather high "entrance fee," your total self, dedicated to God. Some people will be ready to pay the price, others will not, even if the evidence is very convincing.

Christianity has not been tried and found wanting; it has been found difficult and left untried.

G. K. Chesterton

Drinking beer is easy. Trashing your hotel room is easy. But being a Christian, that's a tough call. That's rebellion.

Alice Cooper

Station 13 - Dealing with difficult people

Ok, so what if you're stuck at Level 1 success? You do your best to behave yourself but the other person is... shall we say... a little less gracious? Don't abandon these kinds of conversations too quickly, for some benefits can be gained, many of which are common to Level 2.

[28] Thomas Nagel, in describing his own Atheism, wrote, "It isn't just that I don't believe in God and, naturally, hope that I'm right in my belief. It's that I hope there is no God! I don't want there to be a God; I don't want the universe to be like that."

- Whether you realize it or not, seeds are almost certainly planted. Your friend may uproot them faster than you can plant them, but maybe some will stick.

- Not only do you get a chance to practice you reasoning skills, you probably get a chance to practice spotting fallacious arguments. Usually when people get hot under the collar they immediately shut off their brain. Their arguments suddenly just become quarrels, so it becomes easier to spot their flaws. Of course, be **very** careful how you present those flaws back to them (you should probably wait until they settle down)!

- You get to practice the very difficult skill of remaining calm under pressure. Their blood may be boiling, but make sure yours does not. Remaining calm when people are visibly upset, calling you names and hurling accusations your way is not something you can master overnight. It's not pleasant, but it is important to learn.

- If there are others watching it may be refreshing to show an example of a non-Christian behaving badly while the Christian's behavior is exemplary. This will not go unnoticed; trust me!

If you find yourself in a conversation with a difficult person do everything in your power to change the tone of the conversation without sacrificing Truth in the process. Some people are tempted to back-pedal on their convictions, but resist that urge. As I mentioned previously, one of the rhetorical tactics some people use is to demonize Christians (and others with unpopular views) in order to intimidate Christians into self-censorship so they don't have to do the hard work of defending their own beliefs. Do not fall for that. Stand your ground firmly, but graciously.

However, do what you can, while standing your ground, to gently bring the volume down a few notches, or change the tone of the conversation. I've been surprised how many times another person will start down the road of an unpleasant conversation, and then change their tone when they see that I am not following them down that road. If you keep the volume down and you focus on the facts and Reason it is surprising how many people will follow you down that road, even if they only follow for a little while.

Of course, that will not always happen, so be prepared to put an end to the conversation if needed, but be careful how you do it. I once had a cold call from a Jehovah's Witness who was determined to persuade me of the error of the Trinitarian doctrine.[29] He used several rhetorical tactics on me (condescension, shock and awe, false facts, constant interruptions, etc) and was very much getting on my nerves while I tried to change the tone of the conversation. It wasn't working. Eventually I just told him to never call back and I hung up. Frankly, that was not a bad choice considering the conversation, and I was proud of myself that I kept my cool with him even though I was ready for the punching bag. However, I made the mistake of not getting any of his contact info, so it was impossible to continue the conversation at some other time, if I ever felt like a glutton for punishment.

Also, once again, this shows the importance of talking in person; I bet he would have been a much nicer guy if he wasn't on the other end of a phone.

One last point to keep in mind; some people just want to pick a fight. They are not interested in dialoguing honestly about life's biggest questions, nor is there anything you could say to convince them to consider Christ. Generally it is best to walk away from these "conversations" but even these can be useful for the reasons listed above. If nothing else, you'll get to practice keeping your cool (a very important skill to develop!) and you have the opportunity to show others that Christians do not always back down and disappear when challenged.

Station 14 - Oops, I screwed up

And, of course, if you fail to even attain Level 1 success then you get to practice the fine art of swallowing your pride, owning up to your mistakes,

[29] He found our website, **http://www.whyjesus.ca**, and my name is on there as the primary contact. He must have looked up my number in the phone book or something, because it is not on the website. I don't want to give the impression that Jehovah's Witnesses are now in the habit of cold-calling people.

and offering a sincere apology. Make sure it is sincere, though, none of this, "I'm sorry for what I said, but YOU started it..." nonsense! Apologize without strings attached and without qualifiers. One time, after I had to eat my words and apologize, my friend admitted that he was trying to get a rise out of me! We still talk often, we still disagree, and I think our friendship is better for it. Non-Christians have surprised me in their willingness to forgive, and are often rather impressed with a well-worded, sincere, apology. Even that will serve as a testimony because many people choose not to apologize at all.

Here are a few guidelines for apologies:

- **Don't wait**! This is important. When you realize you messed up, start debriefing immediately, figure out your mistakes, and start preparing your apology right away. Deliver your apology as soon as possible.

- **Be specific about what you are apologizing for**. It would be unreasonable (typically) for you to apologize for holding your beliefs, but very reasonable for you to apologize for how you handled yourself while trying to explain or defend them.

- **Apologize in person**. Ideally, you should speak in person whenever possible, but apologies are definitely best delivered face-to-face.

- **The context of your error should match the context of your apology**. This is a difficult one to live out. Private errors deserve private apologies, but if you err in a public way then you should apologize publicly as well.

- **Be sincere**. As I mentioned before, don't fake it. If you really don't think you did anything wrong (and maybe you didn't) then perhaps it's not an apology that is needed. But if you did screw up then own up to it by first acknowledging it in your own heart and mind.

We will not always succeed, but even failure offers plenty of opportunity for learning. Do not fear failure, but do not go out looking for it either!

Phase 5 - Specific subjects to study

If you jumped straight to this section without reading the rest of this book - STOP.

STOP

STOP

I'm serious, go back, read this book from the beginning. Too many people jump to the "right answers" without learning how to handle the truth - this is like giving a loaded gun to a child. Too many Christians have been more concerned with sharing the truth than they have been with their methods for sharing the truth and as a result many non-Christians have walked away from encounters with Christians ever firmer in their resistance to Jesus!

If you just want to throw the right answers at people then I beg you to stop.

Assuming you have read the rest of this book already, and have taken seriously what is written there, let's proceed. What's the purpose of studying this material? The first, and biggest, purpose is to get a sufficient knowledge of the facts related to a given subject. This will avoid surprises during conversations, and will help you graciously correct ill-informed skeptics of Christianity that you will run into. A second reason to study this material ahead of time is to get a "lay of the land" so you know which aspects of the conversation are really important and which are unnecessary distractions. When you understand the big picture on a given subject that helps you gently guide the conversation through carefully worded questions and knowing which of the errors and misconceptions your friend may believe are worth tackling and which are worth letting slide.

Lastly, as others have observed (and I concur) becoming familiar with the subject at hand also makes it much easier to keep the conversation level-headed and cool. When you see that your viewpoint is under attack, and you realize that you are unable to defend it, the temptation is very strong to use aggression to offset your lack of preparedness. Been there, done that! Knowledge is valuable in its own right, but it also brings with it certain unexpected fringe benefits.

> *I used to be deathly afraid of witnessing and terribly fearful that someone might ask me something about my faith. Whenever I got into any kind of discussion, I was rather defensive and nervous... As I absorb the information and logically understand the foundations for my faith, a calm is resting in my soul... now I understand why I believe, and this has brought me both peace and a non-defensive boldness to witness to others.*

Quoted by J.P. Moreland in "Love Your God With All Your Mind"

Not everybody is going to be an expert on all these subjects; do not feel as though you need to be. The guidelines described earlier in the book will help you navigate just about any subject, even if you have never considered that subject before (though it obviously helps to have researched it!). Just because you don't have a detailed understanding of ALL these areas should not scare you from starting the conversation. However, it would be best to get a decent understanding of at least the following three areas and make sure you have a good, deep, understanding of at least one of them.

- What evidence is there that God exists?

- Why do we believe the Bible is reliable?

- Did Jesus rise from the dead?

Station 15 - General philosophy / worldview

Many people think that educating oneself about Christian worldview should begin with Christian Theology and move out from there. As I described earlier, I think this is completely backwards. Others will disagree, but the way I see it, why should I trust Christian Theology if the Bible itself is untrustworthy? Furthermore, why should I consider whether the Bible is trustworthy about God if I have no good reason to think that God even exists in the first place? In my view, one must start "outside" of Christianity and ask themselves whether it makes sense to move "into" Christianity. This is why Station 15 is quite general and it moves through to Station 17 which is very specific.

As I said, scholars are divided on this point - some agree with my approach and others do not - but that's how I've outlined these subjects. If you don't like this order then just go through it backwards!

Can Truth be known? This is the most basic starting point. Some people claim that the very idea that we can know Truth is already too lofty an ambition. Whether this comes in the form of Agnosticism, Postmodernism or the like, this question is well worth considering as a starting point.

From my experience, though, most people will entertain this idea in vague generalities, but as soon as you dive into any conversation their doubts about the possibility of knowing Truth quickly disappear when faced with the challenge of discovering the Truth. The yearning for Truth is built into everybody, so this is rarely a seriously entertained philosophy.

Does God exist? The most common lines of evidence (or "Arguments for God") tend to be the Cosmological, Teleological and Moral arguments for God's existence. None of these specifically prove Christianity, rather they merely give us grounds to conclude that "somebody" is out there. Familiarize yourself with these arguments. If you study this subject in depth then you will also notice that I only listed three lines of evidence, and even these three are the more "lay level" arguments. There are, in fact, even better arguments out there, and many more of them. If you have trouble wrapping your mind around these (some people struggle with the moral argument) then look into the other ones and find those that resonate with you. Understand them, understand responses to them, and most importantly, learn how to explain them in your own words!

Please understand what these arguments do, and do not, accomplish. They do not PROVE that God exists. They do give us good reason to believe God exists. They do not prove Christianity, per se. They do give us good reason to seriously consider the claims of Christianity. They do not replace Faith. They do provide a rational foundation for Faith. This is the Biblical concept of Faith, anyway; not blind but informed.

Science / Religion. This is a HUGE hot topic these days. Do science and religion conflict? Is it possible to believe in religion and take science seriously? Can we believe in miracles? There is way too much to say on this one, so I will just draw your attention to one of the best resources I have found on this subject from a Christian perspective; the website of John Lennox. Another excellent resource are some of the works of Alvin Plantinga after you have mastered the art of understanding "high level" philosophy. John Polkinghorne has also written extensively on the subject and I am told his works are excellent.

Evolution / Creation. Actually, the bigger challenge you will probably find on this one is within the Christian community, unfortunately. Whatever perspective you take on the subject you will find some Christians who will take great issue with your views. If you accept an old age of the earth then you will be told that you have no respect for the Bible's authority. If you accept a young age of the earth then you will be told that you have no respect for the proper interpretation of the Bible. Both sides claim Science supports their view. If you accept Evolution you will be accused of worshiping science; if you deny it you will be accused of being scientifically illiterate. It is shameful to admit, but the greatest challenge to this discussion is from within the Church, not from without.

Still, there are fundamental questions that needs asking; if "nature alone" is capable of creating and developing all of life, is there room for God? If not, why believe in him? Is nature capable of this task, unaided? These are valid questions and you need to investigate them, particularly with respect to the Atheist tendency to rely on Evolution as the ultimate "anti God" proof.

How can God permit evil/suffering? This still remains that most popular objection to belief in God, from my experience. Frankly, it is a profound question! This is an honest challenge that any Christian (and Jew, and Muslim, etc) should take seriously. Ponder it deeply and read extensively from both sides of the discussion.

Also, don't forget that the whole "problem of evil" is actually a problem for the Atheist as well! I am certain you will come across this as you investigate the topic.

Station 16 - Biblical Reliability

Suppose we arrive at the general sense that "something" or, more correctly "someone" is out there. What reason do we have to trust the Bible on these matters? These next subjects address exactly this general challenge.

Is the Biblical text reliable? It is often claimed that the Bible is corrupt beyond belief. There is simply no way to know what it originally said. One of the primary advocates for this view is a scholar by the name of Dr. Ehrman. Interestingly, an entire website, called the "Ehrman project," has been constructed specifically to respond to his various claims. Reading his books, and perusing that website, should give you a good handle on this subject.

What says Archeology? A particularly hot topic these days is the question of the Exodus. The claim is made that there is no evidence the Jewish nation ever even lived in Egypt, never mind leaving after a string of miraculous signs; millions of them definitely never wandered the desert nor entered Canaan suddenly and aggressively. Take some time to dive into this one. Various claims are also made about other aspects of the Old and New Testament, but frankly the list is shrinking as more and more archeological discoveries are made. Still, you should understand some of the key points of contention and consider how you would respond.

Did Jesus exist? When scholars get asked this question there is almost always a momentary pause as the scholar wrestles to find an answer without bursting into laughter. This is not a serious objection to the Christian Faith, and it almost never really was. [30] Still, some people think the jury is out on this one, so you will need to understand a bit about how scholars engage in ancient history so you can comfortably navigate this objection.

Also keep an eye out for allegations that the stories about Jesus were merely "borrowed" from the myths and legends of other religions. Take the time to investigate which myths were allegedly borrowed, and confirm that the myths actually say what people claim they said. Remember what I said about "false facts" earlier on? That runs rampant here, so do your homework!

Early date for New Testament documents. This is an important point for the reliability of the New Testament documents as history. If the documents were written fairly close to the events they describe, then the possibility that they were tampered with is significantly less than if they were written much later. Most scholars date the entire New Testament to within about 30 - 70 years of the events they describe which, from the perspective of ancient history, is a heart-beat. Understand how they arrive at the dates they do, the issues surrounding why divergent opinions exist, and compare the time gap of other ancient historical records that are accepted as accurate.

Jesus' resurrection. This is one of the grand-daddy subjects. You definitely owe it to yourself to examine the evidence, consider objections, and work your way through the wealth of books, videos and websites dedicated to

[30] As a piece of entertainment, you might want to listen to this Ex-Christian scholar set the record straight for this hard-core Atheist with respect to the fact that Jesus existed. **http://youtu.be/zdqJyk-dtLs**

exploring this subject. Some of the leading Christian experts in this area include William Lane Craig, Gary Habermas, Mike Licona and others. These guys would be a great place to start.

And do not forget to carefully consider the objections. Does the claim that it is merely a borrowed legend make sense? Is it possible that the disciples stole the body? Could Jesus' post-mortem appearances have been nothing more than hallucinations? There are a lot of alternate theories out there, and you owe it to yourself (and friends you discuss this with) to understand these other theories, take them seriously, and consider why they do not hold water. The importance of the fact of Jesus' physical resurrection from the dead as an historical event cannot be overstated. The Apostle Paul certainly did not tap dance around the issue.

And if Christ wasn't raised to life, our message is worthless, and so is your faith.
1 Corinthians 15:14 CEV

Station 17 - Christian Theology

Finally we move into the realm of Christian Theology. This is obviously a monstrously huge subject, so I just picked a few of the key doctrines that are likely to be a problem for somebody considering Christianity.

Trinitarian Doctrine. Let's be honest; this doesn't exactly make sense, does it, even for Christians? Frankly, the concept of three separate individuals who are all part of one God is definitely a mind-job on Christians and non-Christians alike. Some key questions to ask yourself include:

- Does the doctrine constitute a logical impossibility? Does it defy the law of non-contradiction, for instance?

- Is the doctrine Biblical?

- Should we expect the nature of God to be fully comprehensible to humans?

The angry / bloody God of the Old Testament. This is another really hot topic. How could God command the Israelites to slaughter all the people in the land of Canaan. It gets worse. Not only does He command them to engage in war (which might, almost, be understandable), but they were expected to wipe out the women and children too! Even the animals! How does this line up with the concept that "God is love?" These are good questions, and they deserve careful consideration. A recent book specifically on this subject is the book "Is God a Moral Monster?" by Paul Copan, which I have been told is an excellent book.

How can a loving God send people to Hell? If you thought killing the babies was bad, now we talk about Hell. This is another of those very common, and very powerful, objections to Christianity. It's bad enough that God is so selfish about loving ONLY him, but to throw people into Hell just because they never heard of him; that's just wrong, isn't it?

Or is it? Think this one through carefully, because you will almost certainly be confronted with it. In fact more than one friend of mine has told me about conversations where a non-Christian looked them in the eye and asked, "So you think I'm going to Hell?" Yikes! How do you answer that?

Station 18 - Study Tips

Researching subjects is a bit of a science and a lot of art. At first you will probably find that you end up buried in quicksand because every question you answer leads to three new questions. Furthermore, which authorities can you trust and who are the crack-pots? How do you know if you have a sufficiently detailed knowledge of a subject area? There are no set answers to these questions, but here are a few tips to keep in mind.

Keep records. This is absolutely critical, and unfortunately I often fail to heed my own advice. I cannot recall how many times I get in a discussion with somebody, tell them about this book I read or website article I saw that related to the conversation. Then, of course, do you think I can find it again?

Not a chance. Whether you write notes in a journal, save hyperlinks in a research folder, or whatever you do, just find some way of keeping track of what you read, key quotes that impacted / informed you, and so on.

A little knowledge is a dangerous thing. This point is absolutely critical. A study was done that correlated people's perception of their own competence in a given subject with their actual competence relative to "average" people.[31] Quite consistently the people with the least competence had the most over-inflated sense of their abilities relative to the norm. Ironically, the people with the greatest competence tended to underestimate their abilities relative to others. Two lessons. First, if you read only one book, visit only one website, or spend only a little bit of time studying a certain subject you are almost certainly in possession of a "dangerous" level of knowledge. Secondly, if you enter these kinds of conversations feeling pretty smart about the subject under discussion, you are probably about to embarrass yourself. Humility is the order of the day in all cases. Humility, and further study.

Beware the "silver bullet." This is related to the previous point. It is not uncommon to hear claims like, "this one argument demolishes Christianity," or "I can refute Atheism in 2 minutes flat." If you see these kinds of claims about quick, easy and irrefutable evidence or lines of arguments it is nothing more than intellectual bravado. Any conversation worth having will be time consuming, will probably require a great deal of personal research to truly understand, and will end up with a less-than-irrefutable conclusion.

How is this related to the previous point? Simple: people who make these kinds of claims are typically of the "a little knowledge is a dangerous thing" variety. Beware of them and do not imitate them.

Prepare to be wrong. The first non-Christian religion that I researched in some depth was Mormonism. During that process I had to learn the humility of questioning assumptions I held about my own Theology, but had never

---

[31] Unskilled and Unaware of It: How Difficulties in Recognizing One's Own Incompetence Lead to Inflated Self-Assessments. The title really says it all, doesn't it? **http://www.steamfantasy.it/blog/manuali/unskilled_unaware_of_it.pdf**

really researched for myself, nor confirmed whether my understanding was even consistent with the doctrines of my church. Though I have no delusions about Mormonism being generally true, some elements of Mormon doctrine, it turned out, were actually closer to a Biblical understanding than were my own views. Always be prepared to be corrected.

Every discussion has two sides. This is a major theme of this entire book, so I will not belabor the point. Read the perspectives of those who agree with you, absolutely, but the discussion is likely to go much better if you have carefully considered the perspectives of others before they bring it up.

Everybody is biased. This fact seems to elude a lot of people. You are biased. Your friend is biased. Experts are biased. Even the sacred "Scientists" are also biased. There is not a person on the planet who is perfectly neutral on any subject. As you study, always ask yourself what biases any particular author is bringing to their treatment of the subject. Also remember to ask if your own biases are tainting your investigation. Biases do not make it impossible to arrive at truth (as the Postmoderns would have us believe), but it does present a challenge along the journey.

Facts versus Philosophies. This is related to the previous point. Given the universality of human bias, everybody's interpretation of the data will be influenced by their worldview. In each subject there will be the facts of the situation which are the same for everybody, but the interpretation of those facts will depend on the worldview you bring to the conversation.

This is not to say that all interpretations are valid; obviously they are not, otherwise we would still be debating whether the sun truly is at the center of our solar system. Remember that you have two jobs as you research; learn the facts and also learn how one's worldview may be skewing their interpretation of the facts. Or, how is your worldview skewing your interpretation?

Authorities exist for a reason. It is true that authorities can be wrong (it happens a lot), but in their area of expertise it is more likely that they are right than somebody who is not well educated in that area. I recall a Bible study I was involved in where a discussion came up about Old Testament laws. One law pertained to the circumstances wherein a groom might accuse his bride of not being a virgin.[32] The young lady is expected to provide proof of her virginity, which, in certain translations, reads, "tokens of virginity." One couple in our Bible study group was convinced that these tokens were comparable to the currency of choice at amusement parks. They were convinced that young girls were entrusted with these "tokens" early in their childhood, and these tokens were voluntarily handed over when they lost their virginity (hopefully on their wedding night). Many commentaries explain the meaning behind this term of discretion, which I will avoid doing here because it fits into the "too much information" category for me.

The moral of the story? Authorities (like the authors of commentaries) exist for a reason; use them before you embarrass yourself!

Jack of all trades, or master of one? Typically most people have to choose one of two paths. You cannot know everything about everything, so you will either become very familiar with one subject and leave aside others, or you will get a decent handle on a number of different subjects without mastering any of them. There are pros and cons to each.

If you choose to master a single subject then you will be able to very authoritatively address that subject. This is a major advantage, and we need more Christians like this. The down side, obviously, is that as soon as the subject changes then you are now outside your area of expertise.

If you choose to be a jack of all trades then the greatest advantage is your ability to have a reasonably informed conversation with just about anybody on just about any subject. For most people, this will be the more effective strategy. You will be able to carry yourself well with Muslims, Atheists, History buffs, Postmodernists, Science-lovers and so on. The downside, obviously, is that you will inevitably run into people who are more knowledgeable than yourself. The imbalance in expertise will show in the conversation, but people with a specialization in one area are often pleasantly surprised to find somebody else with even a little knowledge in their area,

[32] Deuteronomy 22:13 - 21. That same word, "tokens," is also used on several other translations, but this couple happened to read from the KJV.

especially if that knowledge is combined with humility. Having done some research is far better than having not done any in which case your views will be dismissed out of hand.

No matter which approach you choose, remember that every conversation inevitably leads to a black-hole of ever-expanding questions. One answered question leads to three more unanswered questions. At some point you will need to draw a line in the sand and be content that there will always be holes in your knowledge. Frankly, there will always be holes in any human's knowledge. This is rarely a show stopper in a conversation, so don't sweat the fact that you don't know everything.

Resources

I am a BIG fan of free stuff. Fortunately there is a wealth of high-quality, absolutely free, material to be found on the internet if you know where to look for it. The links below are some of the cream of the crop that I've found, and I hope you will find them equally valuable.

General resource websites

These sites are not affiliated with any particular religion or philosophy, and are useful for just learning about "stuff." Remember what was mentioned previously, though; everybody is biased! Even though this is neither explicitly pro- or anti-Christian it is still human-based and therefore biased.

Wikipedia (**http://en.wikipedia.org**) - This can be a very useful source for an introductory familiarization with a wide range of subjects, but you seriously need to use your discretion here.

Google Scholar (**http://scholar.google.com**) - A bit of a step up from Wikipedia in the sense that you get to access actual scholarly material instead of just trusting that the editors of Wikipedia accurately summarized the information. Much of it is pretty high-end, and even here some of it is questionable.

Stanford Encyclopedia of Philosophy (**http://plato.stanford.edu**) - a great place to learn about all kinds of philosophical stuff. It's pretty "high end" though, so put your thinking caps on.

Philosophy Papers (**http://philpapers.org**) - an absolutely gold-mine of resources related to philosophy. Again, a lot of it is quite "heady" but we aren't in this because it is easy! Some of the material requires payment, but there's still a lot that's free.

iTunesU (available through iTunes) - If you've ever wanted to take post-secondary courses but don't have the time/money, this may be for you. Through iTunes you can find "iTunesU" which provides a wealth of free post-secondary courses in audio and video format.

Fallacies and urban legends:
http://www.logicalfallacies.info/
http://en.wikipedia.org/wiki/List_of_fallacies
http://www.snopes.com

Non-Christian websites

Remember how we should consider the other person's perspective before we attempt to refute it? That's why these sites are listed first.

Atheist
Infidels website (**http://www.infidels.org**) - This is probably the best place to start. Many Atheist websites are not worth the visit, but this one has some good material (and some very bad material, but I digress).

Islam
I must admit, I have not had much opportunity or interest to study Islam. As such, the sites I offer may not be the best, but of all the sites I saw, these looked the most promising.

IslamiCity - (**http://www.islamicity.com**) It appears to offer a good deal of information.

Islam - Christianity (**http://islam-christianity.com**) - This offers Islamic information specifically as it compares to Christianity.

Jehovah's Witness

Watchtower website (**http://watchtower.org**) - The official website

Mormon

LDS website (**http://lds.org**) - The official website

Maxwell Institute (**http://maxwellinstitute.byu.edu**) - Dedicated to researching the veracity of the Book of Mormon (among other subjects).

Christian websites

And, lastly, here are many Christian sites that cover a wide range of subjects related to Christian Theology and Apologetics.

General

Apologetics 315 (**http://www.apologetics315.com**) - probably the single best resource on the internet for finding material related to answering the "why" question for Christianity. Links to a lot of other sites, and subjects are categorized with material under each of them.

Apologetics Search Engine (**http://apologeticssearch.com**) most of the resources below are indexed through this one, powerful (Google-based) search engine.

The Last Seminary (**http://www.lastseminary.com**) - Plenty of Theology and Apologetics articles.

Reasonable Faith (**http://www.reasonablefaith.org**) - Fairly high level work, but some is provided at a popular level.

John Lennox (**http://johnlennox.org**) - Mostly popular level videos about science and Christianity. Very good content; I really love this guy!

Stand to Reason (**http://www.str.org**) - A popular level ministry covering a wide-range of subjects.

Ravi Zacharias International Ministries (**http://rzim.org**) - Primarily focused on the relationship between Faith and Culture, but with some very good material related to defense of the Faith. This is a fabulous site for observing how to have the conversation.

Center for Public Christianity (**http://publicchristianity.org**) - Another popular level site with a lot of good material provided by scholarly sources. Lots of video interviews.

Christian Classics Ethereal Library (**http://www.ccel.org**) - A wealth of classical Christian literature. Just because it's old does not mean it's outdated! (incidentally, that's another fallacy)

Bible skepticism

Ehrman Project (**http://ehrmanproject.com**) - Bart Ehrman has become something of a poster child for Biblical Skepticism. Thus, an entire site dedicated specifically to responding to his claims is a useful repository of information on the subject as a whole. Lots of videos.

Islam

Answering Islam (**http://answering-islam.org**) - Probably the premier website dedicated to exploring Islam from a Christian perspective.

Mormonism/JW

Institute for Religious Research (**http://www.irr.org**) - A wonderful resource dedicated primarily to exploring and responding to Christian "cults" (be very careful when / how you use that word!)

CARM (**http://carm.org**) - Another somewhat general website, but with a focus on the "cults."

Bible Study

E-Sword (**http://www.e-sword.net**) - What I consider to be the best free Bible study software you can download.

Bible Gateway (**http://www.biblegateway.com**) - A great online resource of Bible translations, commentaries and dictionaries if you don't want to download software - like E-sword - on to your machine.

Blue Letter Bible (**http://www.blueletterbible.org**) - Another great online resource, with different strengths and a different focus than Bible Gateway.

Bibliography

Tactics - Greg Koukl
A Rulebook for Arguments - Anthony Weston
Love your God with all your Mind - J. P. Moreland
Is God a Moral Monster? - Paul Copan

Online courses:

- Apologetics and Outreach (Jerram Barrs) - **http://www.lastseminary.com/apologetics-outreach/** - This lecture series is more like an introduction to how to do apologetics than it is about apologetic subject matter specifically. Barrs also describes the intellectual state of our culture and various popular philosophies including Postmodernism.
- Apologetics Survey (Dr. Douglas Groothuis) - **http://www.lastseminary.com/apologetics-survey/** - At the time of this writing I have only finished the first few lectures and already it is promising to be a highly valuable resource.

ABOUT THE AUTHOR

Paul Buller is trained and employed as an engineer, but developed a passion for the big questions later on in life. He is a husband and father of two, and an active participant in Church ministry, especially through the Network of Christian Apologists in Calgary (**www.whyjesus.ca**). He also loves to keep in shape through activities like basketball, hiking and biking. He has his pilot's license and dreams of owning a small airplane one day.

He also finds it very strange to describe himself in the third person.

53292063R00047

Made in the USA
San Bernardino, CA
14 September 2019